Verses of

UTTAM PATI

ZORBA BOOKS

ZORBA BOOKS

Published by Zorba Books, December 2023
Website: www.zorbabooks.com
Email: info@zorbabooks.com

Title: **Verses of Reason**
Author Name: Uttam Pati
Copyright © Uttam Pati
Printbook ISBN :- 978-93-5896-215-4
Ebook ISBN :- 978-93-5896-196-6

Zorba Books Pvt. Ltd. (opc)
Sushant Arcade,
Next to Courtyard Marriot,
Sushant Lok 1, Gurgaon – 122009, India

Printed in India

CONTENTS

EARTH

PLUMERIA

Under the high sun, my senses
are focussed upon the clusters,
in magic, at a distance, in silk
white, glazed, each of them in
smile, with a gold-sprayed heart.

Five petals, perfumed, they
erase the hidden despair, the
sorrow, of unspoken thought;
instil courage, not to be fallen
ever be coated in fragrance.

In the shades of dark leaves,
the encirclement of white, in
smoothness, the non-decayed
hope, ever makes a vow to live,
away from slumber, unbroken.

OTHER SIDE

lying upon the bed,
with layers of memory,
amidst invisible clouds,
no more desires enchant,
its footprints, rescinded.

Windows are shut; the
distant view of hanging
nests, in palm trees, midair,
knits the mind, in a rhyme
of flying, in pause, in dive.

Windows are open; far away,
the wind blows. Weaver birds,
against the blue sky flutter,
pretend, whirl around; the
tiny beaks squeak, in noise.

World, an image of desire,
has no insanity; as long as
I stop this surfing octopus
throw in its tentacles, into
the window, to triumph.

Closed eyes, turn blind,
to the shows, in our world;
of leaves falling, alive, in
swirl, dry, in ancient dyes,
in spreading across the lawn.

An invisible, distant bridge,
entangled, in dots, between
two worlds, of the sky and the
earth, allures me to search
upon its infinite steps, in sleep.

THE JOURNEY

Upon the slope, to the
top, walking past the
trees, them, receding in
to the past, midway before
the apex, a sane thing is
to glare, into the sky.

An insane memory
revives thin blood.
Out of a leftover past,
the scar, a remnant of
an old fiery wound
is to be overlooked.

Every journey changes
the meaning of living.
The sound of a bird's

whistle, of the crushed
leaves, under bare feet,
are a prelude to solitude.

Atop the mountain, the
wind, a softener of silence,
owns a symbolic victory.
I look down, breathe in,
glide upon the ground, in
reviving another dimension.

SHADOW OF WIND

The window accepts the
wind's nudging. From the
inside of my house, one
sees a rising sun, far away
from the whistle of wind.

My two close intruders,
the sun, in orange, and
the wind, in action, they
brush my mind in hope,
in love, in dark and light.

THE TREE

In an assemblage, monks,
in green, meditate upon the
landscapes; inhale the exhaled,
breaths, in purifying others' sins.

In spring, through the petals,
they smile, in infinite colours,
in reflecting joy, passion, in
healing the broken hearts.

At night, they straighten out,
exhausted birds, to rest, snooze.
In secluded dark shades below,
lovers caress, kiss, in hiding.

As the storm arrives, they
tremble in pain, to realize the
tiny birds fall off their nests,
amidst the screeching squirrels.

In winter, they stoop over,
the little girl, who kneeled,
in a frilled frock, in laying a
rose upon her mother's grave.

THE SUN

The sunflower
spins in the ray,
paints itself
in crystal yellow;
adsorbs the smile
of the little girl
in the yellow dress.

Smeared in with
gold, she inhales
more yellow, the
soaking becomes
an immersion, the
essential desire
until the sun sets.

RIVULETS

In gliding upon, in falling
off through the sky, over
the cliffs, trees, roofs, in a slow,
lonely, majestic, dance, water
drops reflect upon, the rhythm.

In awesome movement, a
spherical motion, shining
deep, in mystic symmetry,
as if they are alive, wavy,
in flow, to embrace the earth.

In a distant haze, a smear
in disguise, drops merge upon
the sea; upon the surface,
they flow as rivers, in carrying
ancient, infinite memories.

The movement is the rhyme.
The glow, the lustre, open
to emanate a sense, the flow.
The falling, spreading, in tunes,
enchant me ever, in thought.

Standing by the waterfall, in
a pavilion of infinite, sound,
drops roll upon my face,
resuscitate an urge; send me
back to the world, silently.

FLOWER SHOW

Ever do I feel, how in
touching the sky, trees turn
into curtains. Live cubic prints
in fluorescence, are flowers in
patterns, amidst the slow wind.

Life thus pushes me into the
crowd, in searching for flowers
from the tiny hand of a little boy.

A bunch of white lilies, its wild
fragrance brushes off the debris
of a fractured love. With a low eye
contact, my companion, kisses
the bouquet, smiles, in silence.

At night, I dream of flowers,
in the sky, at no distance. Upon
a precipice, a tiny purple flower
smiles in a whisper, saying life
is ought to be lived in fantasy.

DAY VS NIGHT

The field is parched dry,
coated, in thin yellow grass.
In losing the lost episodes of
the green sensual prints, it
grieves with its gloomy sight.

Days break down, in thirst,
of inconsolable people, the
pets, unsure eyes in fatigue.
They wait, unknowingly, that
night may unpeel new wounds.

Moon's ego, blurred, eclipsed,
in a world of haze in grief, all
sleep in the dark, with no virtue.
Silvery moonlight poses a myth,
the thirst for life, burns in pain.

Morning would be a recluse.
The new sun would be kind.
In reinventing hope, in washing
off the sin, the sky would grace
a rainfall, all would close their eyes.

MONSOON

A slice of the rusted earth
awaits to be wet,
under an alluring stampede
of collapsed clouds.

In the shades of green,
life would change.
The sky that pours in, would
enthuse people to smile.

Kites gobble knotted worms.
Otters, in the river,
float on their back, tiny claws
curled, as artefacts

At night, my moving thoughts,
stand still. In the
silent nuances, of the fireflies
as the shooting stars.

In an echo of existence as
the life sprouts out,
in the absence of, noise, malice
earth turns into heaven.

THE RAIN TIME

The misery is insignificant,
as the sky lands upon earth.
Its millions of tiny feet, inside
the water drops, land upon,
in an insane falling across.

Children in raincoats, jump
and frolic, in splashing around,
in muddy, damp, puddles. The
slim, wet, penguins, kick the
sludge, as if kicking footballs.

Awesome drops fall straight,
bend, twist, in wind, in speed.
With no patience boys and girls
urge to be washed out, blown
away, in a thumping spree.

Years later, boys would grow
up as generous men. Walking
under an umbrella, they would
follow the ladies, avoid the wet
patch, once upon a fun sport.

The rain, the water, the game
the boys play, have thrill. The
time rotates the wheel, of
events, asking men how to deal
with, the colluding, women.

NEIGHBOURHOOD

In one early spring, all
alone, a boy sneaked in
to a fair, across the village,
for a phantasmagoria of
experience, under the sun.

His glassy eyes chased,
reflecting upon people, in
their tight and lose attire,
the turbans, in colour and
white, in a canvas of looks.

He conceived seeing people,
in slow motion, walking
backward, in time, the steps
they traversed, the sequences
that connect them with all.

Near the river, under the
calm trees, all were in a
transient gloss of chaos, no
distance between, without
concern, he stood still.

Breathing free, he roamed
around, whistling, in no
sound; pretended, touching
the people, if they are real
as the true neighbours.

The declining sun mellowed
down the lines, between the
tree clusters, the howls fade.
The boy sensed; time has
ended, for another renewal.

At home, back in the cage,
another vision of a new run,
awaits: a mind-travelling act,
a prelude to a real look, for
more adventure, tomorrow.

THE NILE

At the sunrise, she waives,
through crystal dark eyes.
Of an undulating face,
ivory white, circled
in sky-blue scarf.

Her undeciphered look,
an incomplete reflection,
against mystical pyramids,
has swallowed time;
BlueNile, an ancient flow.

The breaths, surge her
bosoms, against the burning
sun in the kingdom of sand;
she holds the memory of
Cleopatra and her lovers

At the sunset, in pause,
in the parted-zones of time,
she hides, emperors,
gods, aliens, in her ripples,
as the immortal queen.

EARTH

In a glass bowl,
life holds on as the goldfish,
its eyes, wide open, throbs in
its silver gill.

In a storm,
the trees tremble, they would
not break; the fallen ones
would bud out.

An octopus,
in no water, writhes;
it is aware, to inhale
through the skin.

Earth

The newborn,
cries at the strangers,
soon after the
cord is clipped.

Earth's magic wand
plays the same tune, all over,
to nourish, sustain,
for life to flourish.

LIFE

IMAGO

Life, poetry in a glance, is
to be recited, over again. As
long as it is unsung, facing
death may not be sublime.

In flying to heaven, is the
urge, as a butterfly; inside a
dark sheath, to retain; the desire
to escape into the sky, is sense.

It is a caterpillar, to shed its
flesh, unseeing itself in dark, to
absolve from the pain; it waits,
to receive, a call from sky.

At dawn, the sin is washed;
the past is shed, the future
sings, the butterfly rises, to
see, spin gracefully, flutter, fly.

A thirst for flower, nectar, blue-
sky, is high. In the sun, the flowers
fluoresce, smile, bow; the petals
hint the arrival of the newborn.

The rays of freedom, in the air,
the heaven and earth, are one;
The mind and the spirit, a white
circle, ever to twinkle as a star.

THE CHOICE

A story is often told,
about men vs women,
of sly, deceitful looks,
their lies to each other,
the deceit they relish,
of broil in fateful ends.

Between men vs women,
the fake perceptions, of
their displayed cruelty,
that basks in the noise;
a command from no one
would revive any sense.

The sorrow of children
with hurtful breathing,
over dying pets, the pain,
of unfaithful spouses, in a
magnitude of poignance
bounce a will to reckon with.

In midst of winding folly,
a flash moment of truth,
opens dark eyes to glimmer.
In a new, exciting, glimpse, an
effort, to be faithful, loyal, with
no sin, may scribe a new story.

CHAMELEONS

The world wears a black veil, in
the camouflaged design of deceit.
It is knitted out of dark minds, of
sinful rulers, the new chameleons.

As the wind steals breath, out
of citizen's wings, in a show of
garden petals, a lizard, tumbles,
sneers, at its own colour display.

The masked corporate thugs, loot,
tear, spray, people, with stifling
lies, rip them apart, in shredding
pain; subdue, annex their goodwill.

At corners, in flickering war zones,
humans, before the sunrise, borrow
lizard's swagger, in spreading wings,
to hunt the fake chameleons, to death.

NORTH STAR

An assembly of crowd
in generous thoughts,
are often misguided to
justify chaos, as hawks

At uncertain fear,
in a flip of wings, it
might warp, twist,
swallow in, people
in faking up a storm.

To live, people listen
to the fifth symphony,
a concord of sound in
C minor, and C major,
in searching for joy.

A toxic bubble, bursts
an innocent mind, in
listening to a dictator's
hate speech, crying death,
in repulsion for others.

A sudden spark, glows
in the heart, of hope;
the north star, out of
Beethoven's full notes,
erases the evil, to end.

SWEET HOME

Memories in the desert,
a hot air balloon,
float above, frolicking
until fear strikes.

Back home, alone, it
reminds me of my dead pet.
In the air, for a reason,
an echo bounces back.

Across the window, a
cluster of puppies pawing
around mother's belly, in
an awesome drawing.

In life's whirlwind nuances,
the chair, in the room,
never stops rocking, until
a memoir is scripted.

RHYTHM

In running around, one
loses its strength, reduces
the love for the self, fails
to listen, ignores many.

In a response, I intrude
upon to reason with, the
cause of haste, without
pause, the futility, intent.

In truth, the glory is not
admired, if acquired in
stealth. The speed is lively
as none prefers a slow race.

In a twist, an action opts
for rhythm, in slow glance,
as the rose petals spread
glamour, in a simple gesture.

ON A DAY

Consequences are slow; they
never flare up soon. It follows
the sequence, into our dislikes.
Inside a store, one loves if things
dash into the cart; they don't.

The purpose is strange. None is
aware; what would be the dish,
who would skip out. In life's hill,
roaming is obvious as noiseless
warts; people travel to be silent.

Outside the door, they, in eyes
closed, pretend as philanders,
in carrying grocery bags, forget
what they bought, and for whom.
Invisible charm is underplayed.

Home is the shade. It hides behind
the door. Cooking, unlike walking,
  is of the least concern; a wistful
  monologue, is the preferred art.
People are same, they come, leave.

BLIND EYE

The boy I met
has no eyes.
After gasping around,
he asked me not to,
see him, in piercing eyes

At home
my dog at me
did not look.
Sniffing was real
in guessing
what I think.

As my daughter
arrived,
I closed my eyes,
to guessing
where had she been.
She worried, if
I am ageing, backward.

AN ESCAPE

In the landscape of the
living, in a lounge of
reminiscence, imaginary,
unreal people rest in
grace, after sleepless nights.

Sound of voices, eye
movements in pause,
in thought, their hands,
fingers, eyes, are, trusting;
why must they wait.

People may reclaim
themselves, as real.
Not fretting, in silence,
they may opt out,
for looking at none.

An act could be an old
one; for rejuvenating, one
ought to walk over
into the garden, listen to
trees, watch how birds fly.

A SECRET

In denial,
she refused to age,
and marry none
with no desire,
in her eye.

In winter,
she sailed in the sea;
listened to, whale's moan,
mermaid's song,
her eyes turn blue.

In summer,
she climbed the mountain,
where eagles fly,
in feeding birds,
her eyes, in glow.

At sunrise,
the angel she met,
blessed her to see.
Being blind to all,
she left, for none.

THE DAY AFTER

Fake whispers,
in the late evening,
bend the thin air
inside the houses.

People, as snakes
do; eat, curl, coil,
diminish, lie down,
as empty chairs,
until the sunrise.

In the day light, they
show off, in places,
all around, bluffing,
in procuring profits.

They need music, for
the soul, sound, light,
away from sinful acts,
fall asleep, at peace.

THE PORTRAIT

Distance may lose out,
between eyes and the brush.
An artist's pain is painless;
eyes may escape war,
love is there in the
bristles.

Conversion, an event,
is a draining act.
The brush truly hides
the penance of self,
in flattening, the
pretence.

At the ordeal, the
pain is widespread.
Strangers may cry, at the
cause of sorrow. In slow
motion, the brush
palpitates.

The artist is
the witness to the true
act he plays with. At no
distance within, he
becomes the portrait,
of his art.

DARK NIGHT

A running train inside a
dark tunnel, mimics a static
log, for a short spell,
in no sun.

In a closed room, the mind
ought to negotiate, with the
self, as long as the travel ends
under the sun

With no fear during the
journey, the mind would
reinvent, seal the wound, in
healing it soon.

As per life's protocol
all play-acting, must end;
the tunnel would wear out
in to light

A glow in mind is the
fount; in escaping from the
dark belly, one negotiates
to win .

ALCHEMIST

Unlike a dolphin's
musical swim, man's
self-created hate poisons
all his inherited virtue.

Before the next sunrise
the foulness of his anger
broils his little mind in
burning down his lawn.

Inside a dark cave, an
elixir is distilled, in a
green jar, by a tiny man
with his white fingers.

He would spray the nectar
in to the eyes of the cursed;
to swim past the dolphins
in the deep water, as wind.

LIFE

Detachment from fear is
a fearless act. One could
close eyes, and pretend dozing.
In engaging with a comic
rehearsal, it may recede.

In a different moment, one
could be silent, forget how
the face looks; resist sound
of a noisy street, disregard
if it is night or the day.

Fear breeds in the sly
corner of shrinking time. In
eluding the dark secrets of
past, an act of imprecision,
tunes in a fearless living.

LOVE

THE CIRCLE

Life's note,
in the core of heart,
as a sublime dove,
is seen by a few.

To the one
in love, who feels,
love is life,
has seen it all.

THE COMB

In nineteen hundred eleven,
from a tree-laden, riverside, fair,
my grandmother, at seventeen,
had brought a comb; I gave you,
it was made of buffalo horn.

Half a century later, my mother
gifted it to me; I stored it in a
drawer, along with, paper, pencil, your
letters; as you complained about,
the letters carry an uncanny smell.

I combed your hair with it, as you
were asleep in my arms. Waking up,
you accused me of sorcery through
a spell, the comb, in possessing
you, a deceptive blame; it was love.

A MIRROR

Across both sides of the
table between our faces,
at an invisible distance,
a soft perfume, mingled
with the aroma of coffee,
rises out of two glass cups.

Her face, the mirror, half
of it, covered in black hair;
eyes are tuned in with mine.
The wind blows; the mirror,
transforms, into ripples,
in creating a reflection.

An aura emanates, a sweet
smell, bounces upon, by
itself. A chance meeting
has life; in sailing through
the image, I seek time,
distance, a new memory.

THE CAGE

A green parrot,
wishes to be caged.
It is the enchantment,
that shows to all.

The heart,
pumps more, overjoyed.
It is love, may not it
be calmed down,

Love birds,
later, would suffocate.
To cage the heart,
is essential.

HEART

Distance kills,
the desert is too long.
Scaling it over and down,
the sand dunes, to
repeal a sorcerer's spell,
it needs love.

Her gold eyes,
boxed in my heart,
reflect the sun's rays.
As soon they blink,
the spell would vanish.

A CONFESSION

When my mind joins
you, in a blue lake,
our joint body, floats
above, in mellow sun.

Upon the water, we
see our own reflection.
The sky embalms all
except the hidden soul.

In the last act, the truth
smokes out; it winks at
all. The red charcoal
in my heart still burns.

RETURNED

In the grey, winter morning,
she chose to open an ivory
white, tiny box, in avoiding
the shiny, lapis lazuli one.

In thought, the colour of
things may be in black or
white. Away from the eyes,
the shadow rules over shades.

A unified obstinacy, coils
into the game of thinking.
It could change for a reason
if love assumes it to be true.

In spring, the sun's rays,
throws a miracle, in refracting
colours, out of the box, in glow;
her heart bloomed in desire.

The blue box from Kabul,
pulsed, winked, moaned. In
lovelorn air, she wore the old
sapphire ring, to homecoming.

THE HAMMOCK

The evening anchors upon,
in touching the coconut trees.
Across, man-made yellow
lights, in an organized order
of chaos, drunkards sit down.

Sleeveless girls giggle over
silly jokes, across the sultry,
dark, water line; noisy, sizzling
boats, whistle in light, in high
music, against silhouetted girls.

The movement in hammocks,
the silent lovers, their true
selves, in pretence, some noise,
against the slanting moon,
resemble a fake landscape.

All would rather vanish.
The sea would roar, for all.
Memories may sink, the boats
of yesterday. Hammocks keep
floating, empty, without none.

RENEWAL

At the sunset, as the world's
caterwaul recedes, I imagine of
you, upon the terrace; standing,
eyes closed, looking at the sky.

My days end with tired fingers,
in shaking hands, mean people;
their eyebrows, how they wink,
the way they drink from the glass.

Of your curly hair upon the neck,
glittery against the setting sun,
the eyelids, in grace it blinks, I
could smell, your scent in the air.

Of talks, that lost love from past,
is not the future, is silly. A search
for trust, a renewal of the self, is
the wish in searching for old love.

In mornings, I wish to feed birds
in my hand; tend the sunflowers,
they, to look at the sun. You
would hold my face, smile, in calm.

SCORPION'S LOVE

Once upon then, an ill-fated
rendezvous, glossy, piercing,
thirsty, in self-defeat, met a
a delusive end of romance.

In flashback: inside, she had
pulled up a purple, unbuttoned
cashmere cardigan, against the
snowfall, outside the window.

Her brown eyes, below the
unplucked eyebrows, sparkled
in red-framed glass; roved in
a felinely curiosity, for prey.

A tinge of pretension in the air,
her hybrid accent, shows off
her migrant mind; her charming
fingers, mimic pale flower buds.

She recited well, turning on
slowly, the pages in Hamlet,
of politics and violence, in
a medieval drama, herself,
in midst of a selective play.

In a drama of love, she had
left the Mclloyd House, at the
Maritimes, for a warm south;
eyes, that resonated with distrust.

I was intrigued for long, to
realize, if she, in disguise, is
a loving or selfish soul; never
I could decipher the truth.

The colour of deceit is grey,
thrifty, unwoven, as scorpion's
fluorescence to lure the prey;
with fingers as unkind nails.

In life, at each corner of a
winding road, the wind blows
in difference; one could forgive,
swallow deceit, with distant love.

GHOST

In an empty space, she turned
in to a liar; I became a corpse.
The boat with no boatman,
whips itself with twisted wind.

Gasping around the noose, in
chewing the memories of breath,
her lies punctured my neck, the
wound bubbles in bloody deceit.

Deceit is the ghost; she would
wear cobalt-blue lipstick, sucking
her lover's fractured lips, against
the half-moon, jackals howling.

New ghosts would gather on;
unless the lies are hunted upon,
they would escape the graves; me,
the corpse, would be without life.

LOVE

In the spring, the trees turn in
to burnt umber, at your early
departure, across the staircase,
a vented smell of frozen ghosts.

In stretching my eyes through
the windows, of houses, echoed
a sudden bird's flutter; in falling
off a soft white, of swirling feather.

Slowly, as a bird, I fly, over
the corridor, upon the shining
stairs, inhale, a hearty, puff of air,
glancing at your vanishing hair.

Your arrival, at the door, is like a
breath of life; with a sensuous
body perfume, in the air I could
smell, you stood still at the door.

FAREWELL

COFFEE BREAK

Gentle was the
evening. Brewing coffee
needs nerve; inhaling,
in quelling a low mood.

Across the window,
bright red hibiscus,
pushed each other,
the table shines through,
against a setting sun,

In slow motion,
she entered, after a very
long time, thin,
pale-skinned, blue-skirted.

Out of medium-roasted,
moderately-grinded beans,
in all its lightness,
a mutual sipping on, was
more silent,
in translucent cups.

A short symphony,
with three movements,
arrival, look, and thought,
has edge, over its length,

A twirl in the air,
a flush of vented memory,
brought a wind of
mutual, unsettled,
poignance.

Rejoicing of,
the inhaled vapour
with no thought,
of once a mutual consent,
is silence.

A lost time
is un-submissive,
as the cups are empty.
Unlike regrets,
time replaces the past,
with the future,

A glimpse of life
without froth, is relief.
Flowers calm down
at the thought of evening,
before the departure.

FORGOTTEN

It would cause you
good when I depart.
You may cry; I would
hold you in, inside me.

.

In staying in the world,
you will listen to the noise;
touch the wind upon your
face; look over the river,
write stories, for children.

There is nothing to discover.
As the world is a dream,
to draw a sketch, you
will learn to fall asleep.

As you wake up,
you may forget the pencil.
Hence you are safe inside
me, after I am gone.

DISTANT LAND

The house
I buy for you,
before I am gone,
and you being old.

Near the lake,
with no memories,
the blowing wind,
has no speed;
trees do not nod
as postcards.

With a charcoal
in your hand,
before you leave,
you would draw.

Upon the sky, the
tune of your mind,
of new memories,
spiced in old love.

In another world,
we meet in swapping notes,
reclaiming us
as lost and found cats.

LAST WISH

Wrinkles speak,
life is effulgent,
it shines through
past in to future,
with memories,
of people and sky,
time, a true myth.

Wrinkles narrate,
the past elegance,
inability to knit
life's tiny boxes,
gift wrap's refusal
to pack the gift.

Wrinkles dream,
of flowers, the
tender touch,
of baby's finger,
before the leave falls
upon the green grass.

INVISIBLE

Densely stacked,
winter fog, unfossilised,
stole my dog's breath.

Despair that I failed
to swallow it,
I pushed a rock chime,
through a broken pencil.

Shimmering sprinkles of
of dust, is sublime love,
to touch my dog,
in an awesome desire.

WOLF

In game, hunting wolves,
swing their waists.
Their vulgar eyes roll,
in a zigzag circle.
Stuck unto the tree,
is the blood of the deer.

Upon the crushed grass,
across the howling,
over the peaceful, landscape,
the moon shines.

The deer rises
as a gold coil, fire red,
unto the sky;
spit out violence,
in favour of peace.

DEATH

Life is at a pause,
before no one sees,
the magic of death.

In the mountains,
the king eagle,
is not seen flying.

The fearless rabbit,
snoozes upon the grass,
as if death is untrue.

A sudden wind,
spirals into circle
as a shadow of an eagle.

The frightened rabbit,
upon the grass
runs out of breath,

The mouth is open,
with frozen teeth.
A fearful life,
rests in peace.

Life's canvas, is
brushed upon, in the
shadows of death,

DEPARTURE

The man waits.
Upon a soft pillow
the head feels tight,
the neck slanted,
eyes, sharp, straight,
in inward thought.

Time has no scale.
At ease, in pause,
it emits eloquence
in designing events,
to spread living.

Window sees the
moon. The childhood,
mistakes, regrets, are
all forgotten; no time,
in wrapping them all.

In a waiting lounge, a
mind upon the edge, is
an entangled, woollen
ball; the cat is weak
to play with it.

The night is darker,
in layers of events,
physicians leaving,
sincere goodbyes,
eye contact, whispers.

The door is closed.
Breathing is peaceful.
The man has prayer.
The sun would rise.
He won't be there.

FAREWELL

The corpse lies upon the
yet unlit wood, all in wait,
if the first fire, would
ignite the flame.

The grief-stricken air has
a fume with no malice.
Inert, false, that turns into
an imponderable whimper.

Nostrils are plugged in,
with cotton balls to let the
sleep, go deep, peaceful,
mind, hidden, elsewhere.

Life, a multiplying bubble,
wrapped in, eventful
past, of intricate sequences,
inside a sheath of desire.

In germinating another
perception, in a distant tree,
a flare of new breath, would
flower the old stories again.

Milton Keynes UK
Ingram Content Group UK Ltd.
UKHW041026260124
436746UK00001B/32